Book 1

BOB & CODY WOLFF

CODY & BOB IN THE LITTLE TAIL ADVENTURES™

"Let's Go Swimmin'!"

BOB & CODY WOLFF

Published by
Tail Wiggle, LLC
10400 Overland Road, Suite 143
Boise, Idaho, USA 83709

Book Information:
http://CodyAndBob.com

Cody & Bob In The Little Tail Adventures™ Book, Concept, Design, Theme, Name, Likeness and Image Copyright and Trademark by Robert Wolff

COPYRIGHT © 1998–2018
by Robert Wolff

Cody & Bob In The Little Tail Adventures™
Cody & Bob™
Tail Wiggle™

All Rights Reserved. No part of this book may be reproduced or transmitted in any form or by any means without written permission from the author. All copyrights and trademarks are the exclusive property of the author.

Print edition ISBN: 978-1-949653-00-7
eBook edition ISBN: 978-1-949653-01-4
Audio edition ISBN: 978-1-949653-02-1

First printing August 2018
Library of Congress Control Number: 2018908604

"I love to go swimmin'
"And watch my big paws paddlin'
"I think I could swim for all day long,
"Whenever people see me
"They don't know how I do it
"A big flop-eared boy dog
"Swimmin' so fast and being so strong!"

> **My name is Cody and my best friend is Bob.**

We are happy boys and we love to laugh and have fun.

We have been all over the country.

We have met so many nice people and animals.

We have made so many good friends.

And we have so many stories to tell you.

Like the story of "Let's Go Swimmin'!"

Bob and I are the best friends in the world and we always have so much fun doing anything and everything together!

We have so much fun and meet so many wonderful people and animals.

Everywhere we go, there are so many things for us to see, play and do.

I love jumping in the water and swimming like a big boy dog all day long.

It is so much fun being in the water and floating around and moving my big paws forward and back, as I smile and just look around at all the wonderful sights around me.

It feels so good to my little furry coat to feel the cool water on it.

When I was a puppy and Bob and I lived in the land of Idaho, Bob wanted me to learn how to swim.

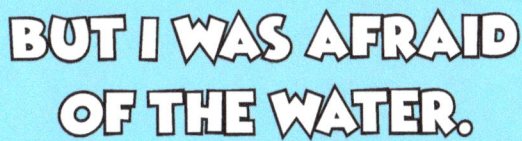

This is where Cody and Bob are!

IDAHO

BUT I WAS AFRAID OF THE WATER.

I didn't know what it was because I had never seen something so funny looking as water!

And whenever Bob would gently push me towards the water and say, "Cody, go swimmin'", I turned and ran away.

Then one day, Bob surprised me.

When we went to the Payette River (it wasn't very deep), Bob gently held me in his hands as he walked slowly out into the river.

Just when I thought we were going to turn around and walk back to the riverbank, Bob lowered his arms and gently tossed me into the water!

Before I could even think about it, my legs were paddling so fast and I was breathing so quickly, that before I knew it...*I was swimming!*

And I was loving it!

HEE...HEE!

From that day on, whenever Bob and I would go bye-bye and I would see water, I would bark and bark so Bob would stop the car and let me out because I wanted to go swimming!

And I love swimming everywhere!

YAY!

I love swimmin' in lakes and when Bob and I lived in the land of Vermont, we would go to Lake Champlain on a hot summer day and jump in the water to cool our big happy boy bodies off.

This is where Cody and Bob are!

VERMONT

HEE...HEE!

The lake in Vermont was so much fun because after 30 or 40 minutes of me swimmin' and dog-paddling, Bob would kneel down in the water, with the sand beneath his feet, and I would swim over to him and just stop and sit down on the top of his leg and both of us would be in the water and we would just relax and enjoy looking at the Adirondack Mountains across the lake in New York.

After a few minutes of me resting on Bob's legs with Bob holding me, giving me good kisses and talking to me, I'd start moving my big paws again 'cause I wanted to do more swimmin'!

I love swimmin' in an ocean too!

HEE...HEE!

When we lived in land of Connecticut, our house was so close to the ocean that it was almost in our backyard!

CONNECTICUT

This is where Cody and Bob are!

Many times, Bob would take me to the ocean and let me run my legs on the sandy beach and with my legs running and my nose down sniffin', I would have the most fun.

YAY!

HEE...HEE!

There's nothing in the world looks like or smells like an ocean!

Oh! I've saved the best story for last!

HEE...HEE!

"I want to tell you the story of one of the funnest times I've ever had and that's when I got to chase the big birds!

HEE...HEE!

So here's what happened...

This is where Cody and Bob are!

NEW YORK

One day, while we were living in the land of New York on Long Island, Bob and I were in the car going bye-bye, and off to the side of our car was a lake and swimming in that lake were birds.

But these weren't small birds.

They were BIG birds that were white, had big long funny looking necks, and made the funniest noises.

HEE...HEE!

When Bob saw how excited I was, he stopped the car and let me out. As fast as I could, I ran to the edge of the lake and then stopped.

The big white birds with the big long necks didn't even see me.

HEE...HEE!

So I *slowly* put one paw into the water and then another, until I was in the water and swimming.

I doggy-paddled for many doggy paddles until I was only *a few feet* away from them!

I was thinking...those big birds are going to let me give them a Cody doggy kiss!

YAY!

Suddenly...as the big white bird began making a loud noise and started flapping his big wings and like the biggest airplane in the sky, his wings slowly lifted his big body out of the water and into the air and he was flying!

I looked up in the air with big wide-open eyes in amazement because I had never ever seen such a big bird flying!

HEE...HEE!

I was barking and telling Mr. Bird, "Please don't go Mr. Bird! Please don't go! You get back here 'cause I want to play!"

HEE...HEE!

A few seconds later, the big bird's wings stopped flapping and he landed right back in the water, but much farther away from me.

So I turned around and started paddling and swimming again just as fast as I could towards him so I could chase him!

HEE...HEE!

And once again, after I got only a few feet away, Mr. Bird started squawking and his wings started flapping and out of the water he went and he was flying once again!

And off to chase him I went!

The whole time I was thinkin'...
"This is so much fun!"

YAY!

HEE...HEE!

As I was swimming towards Mr. Bird, I looked over at Bob watching us and he was laughing so hard and so loud I thought he was going to cry!

And that made me so happy, so I swam faster and faster towards Mr. Bird so we could do it again and again and again!

HEE...HEE!

Bob and I were having so much fun and Mr. Bird was too!

YAY!

It makes my little tail wiggle and gives me a giggle because I just never know when or where I'll do it all again!

HEE...HEE!

Bob and I are the two best buddies and best friends in the world and we always have the biggest and best times and most fun together!

We just love it whenever it's time for our next "Let's Go Swimmin'!"

We love it so much that we even wrote a song about it and it goes like this...

"I love to go swimmin'
"And watch my big paws paddlin'
"I think I could swim for all day long,
"Whenever people see me
"They don't know how I do it
"A big flop-eared boy dog
"Swimmin' so fast and being so strong!"

So stay tuned...

We've got a new story to tell you, so get ready because it will soon be time for the next...

CODY & BOB IN THE LITTLE TAIL ADVENTURES™

WOOF! WOOF!

Tails wags and doggy kisses to you!
Cody & Bob

Tail Wiggle™
Books for Kids

Go ahead and make extra copies of our fun
photo sketches inside your Cody & Bob book and go to
www.CodyandBob.com for free downloads
of all our fun Cody & Bob book photo sketches so you'll always
have plenty to draw on and color!

HAVE FUN!

We love you!
Cody & Bob